When th
an anthology of contemporary
French counter-cultural poetry

edited by

Alan Dent

Cino — p 23 et sq
Cannon — p 37

STACK
BOOKS

In memory of
Tom Walker (1954-2006)

Published 2007
by

STACK
BOOKS

Smokestack Books
PO Box 408, Middlesbrough TS5 6WA
e-mail : info@smokestack-books.co.uk
www.smokestack-books.co.uk

Cover design by James Cianciaruso

Printed by
EPW Print & Design Ltd

ISBN 0-9551061-9-2
ISBN 978-0-955-10619-4

Smokestack Books
gratefully acknowledges the support of
Middlesbrough Borough Council
and Arts Council North East

Smokestack Books is a member of
Independent Northern Publishers
www.northernpublishers.co.uk
and is represented by Inpress Ltd
www.inpressbooks.co.uk

The editor gratefully acknowledges the invaluable help of
Bob Dixon in translating the poems of Francis Combes. All
other translations are by Alan Dent.

Contents

Gerard Noiret
The Lovers
Silence and Dust
Poor Tropics
Low Tide
Ground Level
Homage to Kundera
From a Mirage
From a Cantata
Song of Pandemic
Zone

Laure Limongi
Relationship(s) VI
from Southern hemisphere
from That life is a dream

Georges Hassomeris
Two Popular Songs :
      What We Have Gained from Bourgeois Democracy
      The Disturbances in the Publishing Sector
What is Poetry ?
Clear Thinking is the Height of Perfection
Comrades, We Are All Concerned !!!
In the Beginning was the Verb

Introduction

In 2006 the offices of *Le Temps des Cerises* were burgled. A number of computer-disks were stolen, containing poetry. Who could have been responsible? Presumably not the 'scum' which Nicolas Sarkozy threatened to power-clean from the streets of Paris. *Le Temps des Cerises* was founded and is run by Francis Combes, the outstanding talent of radical contemporary French poetry. All the poets in this volume have a connection to Combes or to *Le Temps des Cerises*. They are radical, counter-cultural. They are sufficiently well-known and influential for somebody to think it worthwhile raiding the offices of an independent publishing house to steal their work. What are the authorities afraid of? Perhaps this collection provides an answer. These poets are subversive in the best, creative sense. Their work is open to possibility, democratic, joyous, questioning, impatient of pomposity and the empty strutting of rank. They form a community. And their books have a real audience. They aren't best sellers, but serious readers looking for something outside *official* poetry know where to look.

The poets assembled here speak for the unheard. They are the heirs of Chénier, Prévert, Apollinaire, Jarry, Brassens, Aragon. In age they range from the young David Dumortier to the veteran Jacques Gaucheron. There is nothing like *Le Temps des Cerises* or the poets grouped around it in contemporary Britain. It's a characteristically French phenomenon. Most of these writers have never before appeared in English. Translations of poetry are becoming rarer and rarer on English shelves. In introducing these writers to an English audience, it's hoped they will find a permanent place in the minds of readers.

In 1917, a show of Negro sculpture at the Paul Guillaume gallery prompted Apollinaire to write in the review *Nord-Sud*, of the 'audacity in taste which accepted these objects as works of art.' Shortly afterwards in the preface to Parade, he was to speak of 'a sort of sur-realism in which I see the point of departure for a series of manifestations of that New Spirit which….promises to modify the arts and the conduct of life from top to bottom in universal joyousness.' By this time, Apollinaire had already suffered his head wound in the trenches and had begun to exhibit changes in personality and behaviour. Like him, the century had suffered a terrible wound, and like him, one from which it would never fully recover. As Apollinaire wrote :

9

By destroying liberty, this war which the Germans made inevitable arouses our curiosity about people in earlier ages who could live as they liked. The conditions which such an existence requires have never been met as in the 18th century. We can well fear that, after the peace, these conditions may never return, and that regimented men sealed off inside their nationalities, races, professional and political groups, men organized in docile herds, may never again dream that there was a time when one could do what one wanted.

Nevertheless, in the brief period of *Shattuck's Banquet Years*, a handful of bohemian artists in Paris had opened up a cultural space typified by the 'plasticity' Apollinaire loved so much. This plasticity was the counterpoint to the very social freedom whose tone it appeared to replicate and propose. An assault on the bourgeois myth of the isolated individual, it was at the same time the highest defence of individual freedom. Rooted in the paradox that our individual identity is socially mediated, Apollinaire's pursuit of the greatest possible degree of liberty in the arts was also the pursuit of a society courageous enough to loosen its grip on individuals and admit the kind of variety and innovation which had given rise to Rousseau's recovery of innocence in painting, Satie's musical jokes, Jarry's outrageousness and Picasso and Braque's subversive cubism. Illegitimate, uncertain of his paternity, a foreigner, Apollinaire was *forced* to question his identity and to seek to create one out of the materials available to him. Out of this questioning came the insight that our identity itself is extraordinarily plastic.

For Apollinaire, this was a liberation. For the twentieth century, it was a source of fear, panic, neurosis and brutality. Apollinaire's prediction of 'regimented men' and 'docile herds' came to pass ; the forces of conformity, joylessness, petty place-seeking, time-serving and money-grubbing, with all the power of the jack-booted, bowler-hatted, stiff-upper-lipped State at their disposal, killed off his belief in 'universal joyousness' (the kind of unchained formulation he loved as a rejection of prissy, pusillanimous academic or political language).

Inevitably, the spirit Apollinaire had infused into French poetry couldn't last as the conditions which made it possible disappeared. Plasticity of identity with all its suggestions of possibility, found itself frozen out by the need for fixed identities which could serve business, militarism, the State and the world view underpinning them. The First World War left young artists and intellectuals disgusted and in revolt against the values that had given rise to it or failed to prevent it. Paul Eluard and Louis

Aragon, who were to exercise such enormous influence over the poetry of their century, were drawn, in the early 1920s to the suggestive, expansive power of surrealism ; its insistence on the importance of dream, its refusal to adhere to the stultifying norms of conventional life. Later they embraced communism, to which they both adhered so devoutly they were blind to the brutality of Stalin. The allegiance of major poets to a party of doctrine diminished the sense of plasticity and possibility which had promised so much. In its place came a poetry less experimental, less inclined to undermine itself in order to recreate itself, and though of the highest technical accomplishment, simply less joyous. Apollinaire's doctrine was change, experiment, fluidity, transformation, plasticity, lack of fixity, infinity of potential. It embraced no teleology. Poetry allied to a teleological perspective inevitably became more constrained. The simple arrangement of the poem on the page, which Apollinaire had seen as a rich source of experiment, became much more predictable.

There was, however, Jacques Prévert. Having broken with the Surrealists in protest at Breton's authoritarianism, Prévert proceeded to attack the powerful, whether in business, the State, the military or the clergy; sided with the underdog and evoked a gentle and unassuming sense of tolerance, playfulness, friendliness and joy. Somehow, out of this admixture emerges a warm poetry in defence of the cold idea of justice. Prévert is perhaps the most genuinely subversive poet of twentieth century France. Allied to no political party or self-conscious ideology he had an unerring sense for every nuance of arrogance, high-handedness, absence of democracy and spiked them deliciously. As innocent as Rousseau, as jokey as Satie, he is pre-eminently the poet of the democratic sensibility. Elaborating a surface simplicity he managed to attract a wide readership for work which deals with tragic complexities without being daunting. Born in 1900 and publishing his first collections in the mid forties, Prévert was fighting hard to keep alive some of the liberating sense of contingency which Apollinaire had intuited in the conditions of the early twentieth century, but he was fighting against Fascism, collaborationism and occupation. He was inevitably more cautious, discrete and aware of the perils of standing for democracy and, especially, fluidity of identity, against such odds.

After the Second World War, however, there appeared a regressive, mystical strain in French poetry. The useless slaughter of the First World War, the rise of Fascism and the intellectual winter of the Cold War, had all helped to destroy confidence in the belief in secular salvation which, since the Enlightenment, had provided the hope that by understanding and modifying our circumstances we could escape the evils of poverty, war, violence and social breakdown: 'regimented men' and 'docile herds'. This collapse in the belief that materialist explanations could provide both a satisfying intellectual and moral framework and a guide to action, inevitably pushed people in the direction of 'mystical' compensations.

The chief exponent of this in poetry was Yves Bonnefoy. Where Prévert and his predecessors took for granted language's ability to gain purchase on reality, the starting point of Bonnefoy's work is his belief that reality lies in a 'unity' and a 'mysticism' beyond language :

> To have a world, through the word, is to have nothing, to be nothing. To perceive the nothingness within, in the syncope of the word, is to be, by the mere fact of not being. The meanings contribute no more to the mystery of poetry than theologies invoke faith.....words are simultaneously sound and meaning. Where does this paradox lie ? Well, when we perceive words as meaning, as means of communication, we use them to interpret aspects of perceivable reality, or existence, and in this way we construct the world that we live in, but at the same time we detect something in their sound, the noise they make, that is totally extraneous to what we can think or say, and this sound, this eruption can then drag us into its core as can the contemplation of a mass of shapeless stone or the starry sky at night. Over and above all that we think, we know the harsh sound allows us to perceive reality as it exists beyond the confines of our knowledge, a reality that has not been penetrated by the word and is consequently a unity: in short, an experience of the unity or what we term the mystical...

This depressing farrago of misconceptions has given rise in Bonnefoy's poetry to work which appears to resolutely refuse mere meaning in order to seek 'presence' and in doing so fails to maintain much recognisable connection to lived experience or meaning. Bonnefoy's stance, essentially, is that there is no *materialist* explanation for the co-existence of sound and sense. He has staked everything on his assertion that sound and sense are utterly unconnected and that sense is about mere surfaces while sound points to the realm of 'unity' and 'mysticism'. In the putatively meaningless sounds of words he finds an access to the realm of 'unity'. Bonnefoy seeks to get behind the agreement of a linguistic community to embody these arbitrary signs with meaning in order to discover the realm of *absolute* truth, or unity, beyond it. He refuses to accept the *contingent* nature of meaning. In doing so, he denies the very essence of being human. Everything human is contingent, as Apollinaire knew and celebrated. The sounds of words are *not* arbitrary, but often mirror meaning precisely because of the communication between the parts of the brain responsible for the different elements that make up speech. Where Apollinaire was full of confidence in the new discoveries, inventions, movements and above all the new form of *identity* the modern world makes possible, Bonnefoy retreated from material reality to seek an identity beyond the surface of the material world as it exists and beyond the mere meaning of the words which evoke that surface. The most influential French poet of the second half of the twentieth century, Bonnefoy's legacy is a poetry which shrinks from the touch of material reality like Blanche Dubois before Stanley Kowalski.

The poets represented in this anthology are 'protestataire'. One way or another, they are uncomfortable with contemporary reality and kick against the pricks. That makes them much more the children of Apollinaire than the offspring of Bonnefoy. As Randolphe Bourne remarked, 'malcontentedness can be the beginning of promise.' What excited Apollinaire was the promise of a more fluid and varied life offered by the twentieth century's new conditions. The practice of the poets featured here is rooted in the conviction that language not only gains purchase on reality, but that it can change consciousness and in so doing transform reality. Far from seeing the meaning of words as *mere* communication, a matter of surfaces behind which lies a further, more substantial reality, they begin from the recognition of the social nature of language and understand that how we speak of ourselves and others defines what we and they are. Language has the power to wound and heal. Though our primary thinking is in images, language is the means by which those images are shared, the way we establish our common, social view of the world. The way we conceive of ourselves and the world determines the way we act. Poetry is the intervention of language, in a very deliberate and self-conscious way, in that conception.

The oldest writer in this volume is Jacques Gaucheron, born in 1920. Now living in La Frette in a house he built with his own hands, he was raised in Chartres. His father was badly injured in the First World War, and Gaucheron's horror of this left him with a powerful aversion to the stupidity of war. Exiled during the Occupation, he was active in the Resistance and in the atmosphere of intellectual and cultural renewal after the war, encountering Aragon, Eluard, Tzara and others in the National Writers' Committee. The poems translated here are all taken from *Etat De Veille*, published by *Le Temps des Cerises* in 1998. In the introduction to this collection, Gaucheron wrote, 'Poetry has a duty to be vigilant as it has a duty to celebrate.' These two poles - vigilance and celebration - are characteristic of his approach. Ever attentive to the outstanding horrors of twentieth-century history, he is determined to keep in focus what he calls 'humanity's most acceptable face.' Avoiding the twin traps of naïve optimism and deadly cynicism, Gaucheron writes out of the maelstrom of his time without ever letting go of the hope of less manic circumstances. Typical of this is the short poem *A Charming Little Square* which evokes an actual event in which Gaucheron was attacked on the street by fascists while selling copies of *L'Humanité*. A small event in terms of the unconscionable atrocities of his epoch, but nonetheless nasty. Carefully structured to make the charm of the quiet Sunday square the beginning and end of the poem, the piece therefore keeps alive the hope that charm, peace, beauty can ultimately appeal more to the human mind than violence, power and viciousness. At the same time, the ordinariness of the violence reminds us of the need for vigilance about humanity's least acceptable face. Gaucheron's poems pay no homage to political dogma. Their adherence is to an urban, cosmopolitan, materialist sensibility as alert to the ever-at-hand possibility of barbarism as it is to the hope of a breakthrough to economic democracy and social peace. Gaucheron's artistic and intellectual contribution marks him out as a unique voice of the counter culture, destined to endure beyond the prevailing dubious hierarchies of significance.

Andre Frenaud (1907-1993), a major French poet of the second half of the twentieth century, is one of the antecedents recognised by Gerard Noiret, born in 1948 and living in Argenteuil. Frenaud is famous for having kept his distance from any organised movement or doctrine. Interested in Structuralism and Existentialism, he refused to embrace either and was one of the few liberal intellectuals in France to predict and reject the consequences of Stalinism. Like him, Noiret is a poet interested in social realities who has kept his distance from groups or creeds. Attracted by the materialist outlook of Francis Ponge (1899-1988) he admits to an eclectic set of influences: Claudel, Cendrars, Camus, Follain, Guillevic and to an affinity with the work of Franck Venaille, Andre Velter, Francois Boddaert, Pascal Commere, Pascal Boulanger as well as artistic admiration for Esteban, Rossi, Ray, Benezet and Marie Etienne.

Acutely aware of the poet's need to respect language above all, he has said that 'the smallest change of perspective leads you to a different vision.' This minute attention to the angle of a poem is evident throughout Noiret's work. His poems are focused as if by the acute eye of a dispassionate and expert photographer working in black and white. Yet what they picture is the everyday world, the world of banal social realities. It is the enormous respect Noiret pays to this reality, and to the most apparently insignificant of the actors within it which constitutes the moral vision of his work.

Writing in *L'Humanité*, Denis Fernandez Rexatala has said: 'Georges Hassomeris is a great poet who has the charm to squander his talent out of politeness.' It's an interesting notion, the bad manners of conventional ambition. Hassomeris is keen to keep at bay that sense of himself as special, of the poet as a privileged individual, a spiritual presence, the magician of a dark art. All his work drives in the direction of divesting himself of these pretensions. There is more about him of the court jester, of Lear's fool offering snippets of subversive insight to a world that has lost its wits. But however insightful he may be, he wears his wisdom and his learning very lightly. His work is full of techniques whose purpose is to undermine the self-conscious importance of poetry. The ponderous weight of the poet's self-obsessed persona is undercut by orthographic, textual, word and idea play which refuses to separate humanising humour from the most serious issues.

Hassomeris has absorbed some the outrageousness of the Surrealists (although, as a Franco-Greek, he radically disagrees with Breton's contention that Greek culture has occupied Europe for too long and needs to be ousted) and is full of Apollinaire's spirit of invention and playfulness. If any contemporary French poet has kept alive the sense of the plasticity of identity, it's Hassomeris. Unapologetic in his poetic assaults on the stupidity of our economic and political system, he repudiates that genuflecting sycophancy before established authority and dogma which can creep into the work of poets attentive to their place in the pecking order. At times he makes his work look extraordinarily simple, but behind it is always the skill and deftness of a very fine writer. He has the overriding virtue that however perilous, serious or tragic the subjects he treats, he can always make you laugh or smile and you never put down a Hassomeris poem without feeling a small surge of love for life, despite all its difficulties and horrors.

Laure Limongi writes poems and prose poems whose technique is dislocation. She is determined to make strange the better to illuminate the ordinary and has in common with Veronique Vassiliou a *faux-naif* stance intended to disarm. Much of her prose is unpunctuated. Its layout creates the expectation of logical progression but her words constantly turn back on themselves and create the density that is one of poetry's strengths. Part of what her work evokes is the difficulty of inserting a female sensibility into the masculine tradition of French poetry.

Vassiliou's work touches on the same difficulty. She likes to make use of an apparently strict and cold logic which undermines itself by steady accumulations of contradiction. At its best, this technique rises to laughable absurdity. What Vassiliou seems to be doing is pointing to the rationality of emotion. Both these young poets spike the distortion of culture which arises from masculine domination. Avoiding stridency they gently insinuate feminine sensibility into the fissures of contemporary culture to suggest the transformation of our ways of thinking, feeling and behaving that will prevail when men and women genuinely encounter one another a equals. In the case of Vassiliou, this is achieved also by evoking the history and pre-history of humanity and toying with supposedly stable definitions like 'savage'. In a poetry still dominated by male voices, Limongi and Vassiliou point towards a literature more at ease with the subtle and enlivening differences between genders.

David Dumortier works in psychiatry but is also a student of Arab culture and language in Paris, where he now lives. His first collection was published in 2000 and he has published five in total, the last being *Croquis de Metro* from which the pieces assembled here are drawn. These snapshot poems are ironic, witty, wry, touching comments on the nature of modern life. What better milieu, then, than the Metro, that democratic labyrinth where, for the simple purpose of moving from A to B, merchant bankers rub shoulders with bag-ladies? Dumortier's technique is reverse-epic: where the epic expands as a means of embracing and touching on the greatest variety of human experience, Dumortier achieves the same effect through concentration. This part of his work grows from our innate ability to read one another's behaviour. In the smallest signals we can discern the essence of a person's character. In the sardine can of a Metro carriage, in the moving people museum of its corridors, the fleeting encounters with thousands of strangers provide a living montage through which the intensely, minutely social nature of our identity is endlessly revealed. It is this familiarity within strangeness, an experience provided uniquely by urban life, that Dumortier mines for its power to exude meaning and interest. It is in the inexhaustible interplay of strangeness and familiarity that he discovers the epiphanies of significance which he can encapsulate in short, carefully structured pieces which make use of the very same interplay within language. There is something in this of Beckett's intent to hone art from a small arena of experience usually ignored and considered inappropriate for the writer. Tragedy, pathos, comedy, farce, they are all present in Dumortier's miniatures, but they present themselves modestly, unselfconsciously, obliquely.

Francoise Coulmin is a painter and geographer as well as a poet. She has taught the plastic arts at the University of Caen. Her first collection, Pour Durer, from which some of the poems here are taken, was published in 1993. In a sense, her vision is perhaps the most advanced of the poets in this anthology in that she has assimilated a perspective on our status drawn from the insights and discoveries of anthropology and archaeology which leads to a thorough deflating of hubris and the clear positioning of our species as a product of the evolution and natural selection which make us small, vulnerable and temporary occupants of a planet created by blank physical forces at work long before we appeared as they will be long after we are gone. The originality of her work lies in part in its subtle but radical reappraisal of what, for want of a better term, might be called our metaphysics. The existential reworking of our condition is, of course, old hat; but the scientific rather than philosophical basis of Coulmin's perspective renders it, ironically, more poignant and calls, perhaps surprisingly, for greater modesty and compassion. At the heart of her work exists a little avalanche of species pride and arrogance which as it falls away leaves us revealed as in need more than anything of species pity. As Marx identified humanity's capacity for self-exploitation, Coulmin pinpoints our need for self-compassion. Her *Lucy* sequence evokes the sense of our common ancestry, our shared biological heritage and by focusing intently on the facts of our origins strips away the comforting cultural confabulations which admit grandiose notions of our privileged place in the universe. In making us aware of the perilously accidental path we have travelled, she evokes the dangers ahead unless we adjust our view of ourselves to the reality (as far as we know it) of our status as contingent flesh cast up by forces beyond both our knowledge and control.

Francis Combes, poet, novelist, dramatist, translator and moving force behind the publishing house *Le Temps des Cerises*, made this anthology possible by his generous help and advice. Most of the poems translated here are drawn from his collection Cause Commune in which he rings the changes, through a richness of cultural references on the theme of the social nature of our institutions, values, ideas, identity and their historical transformation as we change our circumstances and our changed by them. The influence of Marx is obvious yet it might be misleading to label Combes a Marxist poet. It would be truer to say that he has drawn from Marx the recognition that 'consciousness is an attribute of highly organised matter' and that human consciousness, beyond the bare, wired-in capacity, is neither given nor immutable but reveals itself to be context specific. Intent on detailed focus on precise context, Combes deploys his fascinating knowledge of history, anthropology, literature to examine how particular circumstances have given rise to particular behaviours and beliefs, all the while pointing up the contingent and avoidable nature of the circumstances of injustice to revivify the hope of change for the better.

In *Cause Commune* you'll find poems about Democritus, Socrates, Spartacus, Horace, Christ, Caesar, Thomas More, Marat, Babeuf, Toussaint Louverture , Fourier, Flora Tristan, Nelson Mandela, Blanqui, Jean Jaures, Gramsci, Rosa Luxemburg, Myakovsky, Earl Browder, Trotsky, Diderot. One of the joys of reading Francis Combes is the contact with an encyclopaedic mind. To this he adds a story-teller's ease in leading the reader forward into little narratives, often about the lives and adventures of historical figures. On the other hand, he can concentrate and simplify as in 'Epode On The Natural Order', in which he evokes the major epochs of human history to show how their practices and values were assumed as natural by the people who lived through them, just as our practices and values will look equally odd when change has wrought new circumstances which will subvert much that we take for granted. What emerges from Combes's poetry is a creative perspective on contemporary reality which places it in proper relation to a known past and a possible future; a perspective, therefore, very different from that which prevails in much modern poetry in which an insertion in the present, deprived of much sense of historical perspective, is the norm. Francis Combes has published seventeen books. He is a hugely energetic and productive force in contemporary French, and therefore European, writing. That he is virtually unknown in this country is an idiocy and a scandal. Let's hope a British publisher soon has the imagination to commission a translation of *Cause Commune*. It's a major book, as Combes is a major writer, and English readers should have access to it.

Alan Dent

Metro Sketches

The cold drinks machines
Work 24/24
A useless service:
the metro is closed at night

In a period of bomb attacks
The first thing they protect is the litter bins

A woman makes the best of her reflection in the glass
To straighten her hair:
The world is a little more as it should be after this gesture

The beggar
with the golden teeth
Feeds her treasure
in her arms

A tramp with a litre of wine in his hand,
The police arrest him
Because if they leave him alone
He will plant his vine in the earth.

Sitting on the folding seats
You can look at the backsides
Of the folk standing
Without meaning to.

The peanut vendor
Has had the idea
That people will fancy peanuts today.

A pickpocket has his hands so much
In others' pockets
That his own are always cold.

A man
Has a beard
An astrakhan hat
An overcoat with a fur collar
So much hair above his penis !

By looking at people's shoes
You can know what season it is
Without needing to go outside.

The beggar's body
Has a buttock missing:
In the hollow
The bomb exploded.

The escalators help us
To get ahead.

When you've missed the last train
You reproach it for being on time.
What a pig !

The ticket inspectors will be happy
When everyone is honest
They will be able, at last, to no longer come to work.

It doesn't snow in the stations
The tiles are naturally white.

Sometimes, on the platform, a man goes off the rails.

A veiled woman lowers her eyes
Like a woman naked in front of everybody

A foreigner didn't have a ticket
Fine
He had no identification documents
Arrest
That's how it is
A simple check.

A woman is wearing gloves
Of blue leather
The animal must have been very afraid
When they cut its throat.

At Louis Blanc
They've built on the platform
A glass shelter with three seats
Although it never rains here.

Before the metro
there were moles
This memory is part
of prehistory.

        In the hermetically sealed tin
        A sardine beats its tail:
        A sign that there are still little spaces
        To wriggle in.

On strike days
The human tide doesn't stray far
from home
And the sand stays in the depot.

        The tunnels would close themselves up
        If the trains didn't maintain the holes.

When the metro is free
Fraudsters will disappear at once
As if they had been warned !
Yipee !
We're on our way to zero tolerance !

18 March 1871

It was at dawn on the Butte, just as Paris was rousing
when the milkman's churns clink in women's hands
and the carriers go down to the wine merchants,
it was at dawn on 18th the handiwork was found out.
Making the best of the night,
the commanders sent their troops to occupy the district
and like thieves they seized the canon.
With their bare hands
they brought from obscure corners of the Butte
twenty pieces of artillery,
but half-way down
the alarm was raised
the first national guard gathered at Chateau Rouge.
Louise came down, her rifle beneath her coat
and began to shout;
one after another
the women opened their shutters, their windows
and assembled outside in the troubled early morning air.
Suddenly the tocsin sounded and through the streets
where the drums were beating out the call
the crowds began to stream from all corners of Montmartre.
Soon the troops were surrounded by men, women and
children in thousands, who overwhelmed them
and prevented them going forward
a huge, peaceful and threatening crowd
climbing on the canon, hailing the officers,
fraternising with the soldiers,
a crowd like the sea at high tide,
a stationary swell noisy and various
a powerful and determined crowd
which, without violence, or almost, took back its canon.
(In a Marais garden that day
two officers only would be shot).

In the sky the March clouds rolled,
warlike and joyous clouds,
a gentle sun gilded the fraternal mouths of the canon.
Without planning and by a simple movement
of self-defence
　　　　the people had risen in revolution.
And the members of the Central Committee,
out of their beds,
came to meet the new masters of the city.
Mars had appeared in the heart of Paris
and he turned the sun-drenched heads
of the terrible and the pacific
(beginnings are often terrible and pacific)
like the giant wheels of a flower-strewn chariot.
The clouds rose over the Butte's shoulder
and hurried down to meet the procession of victors
on their way back up
hauling their trophies.
Thiers and his crowd decamped and hid at Versailles.
Paris imprisoned,
Paris besieged
was going to give to the world
the example of freedom.
Paris, victor today and tomorrow martyred
was going to bequeath to the world
the dream of the socialist Republic of free citizens
the great fraternal Federation of communes.

The Lost Tribe

When the Europeans discovered America
the Indians discovered commerce.
They who had never lived off anything
but hunting, fishing and agriculture
learned to hunt the coats of the otter, the wapiti
and the beaver
to sell them to white traders.
'The beaver,' says the proverb,
'is good for lots of things:
cauldrons, knives, mirrors, bradawls.'
And as the White Men were very numerous
and they needed many skins
because they live in an icy, misty place
where you need to stay wrapped up;
they had to give up fishing and growing
and devote themselves to skins
ever more skins
to be stripped off and prepared
and to bring in less and less.
A Seminole tribe
living on the Florida coast
realising they were being robbed
one day decided to do without middlemen.
So all of them
men, women and children,
piled their produce in long canoes
and set off at high tide for the White Man's country
which must be hidden, there,
just over the horizon.
No-one came back.
Victims, among others, of the discovery of capitalism.

NY. N.Y. 9.11

A plane in the sky, which banks on its wing with the slowness
   of a shark
in the middle of the blue skies of the telly screen.
Everybody on Earth, as usual, had their eyes fixed on
Olympus:
a restaurant with a view over the Hudson, a swimming-pool full
of clouds
   on the top floor
the white warriors of the Stock Exchange are seated around
   their oval table.
(They throw their missiles like paper aeroplanes onto the world
not thinking that somebody could do the same to them)
at that height, crystals form in the heart.

High pressure over New York
('it's a good day to die'
says the old sachem
on the television).

When people saw
   (at the same instant all around the Earth)
     the first plane smash into the tower
they at first thought it was an accident.
The net of neurons of the radar screens and towers
   must have broken down.
Then the other plane arrived.
And the towers of the World Trade Center were brought to their
knees
but it was too late to pray
and Manhattan disappeared in a cloud of smoke
like an octopus which hides in its cloud of ink.
(That, every one of us saw.)

By crashing into the towers
the planes brought to the ground the totems
that the white warriors had set up at the tip of the island
and that day
(a beautiful day of blue skies over the town)
death was invited to the table.

Return to sender
the desert storm has retraced its steps
the winds blow right round the Earth
and whoever sows the wind reaps the whirlwind.
The empire is at war
the masters of the world have set free from their box
the demons under their command which slept in the dark.

Every day, hordes of bats gather at the summit of the towers
they take their flight and spread in swarms to the four corners
    of the world.

To liberate yourselves, realize your fantasies ! repeats the
psychoanalyst
    of 5th Avenue.
For years the United States of America has sent us their televised
                                                nightmares
they are the first producers of horror films in the world
and now the bad dreams of their film merchants
are incarnated and return to them full in the face.
(You shouldn't play with dreams.)
In the panic which followed, we saw a dazed woman
who wandered in the street covered from head to foot by a veil
    of yellow dust
similar to the veiled women elsewhere
one among millions of others
a victim of war.

In the middle of the avenues of shattered asphalt
close to the barriers hastily put up by the fire-fighters
silent ghosts passed
whose invisible image was not imprinted on the screen
(they simply made something like a trembling of heat in the air)
the dead of Vietnam, the dead of Chile, the dead of Indonesia,
the dead of Panama, the dead of Ruanda,
Palestinians caught in the trap of the 'final solution',
the dead of Yugoslavia
the children of Iraq
for whom the television
does not bestir itself.

They are all there, filing past unhurriedly
as in one of those films where the clocks stop
when the extra-terrestrials descend on the Earth
and they pass amongst the ruins
indifferent to the drama.

But business picks up again
newspapers dated 11 September sell for as much as 200 dollars
in the hours which follow, an internet site opens
to offer the rubble of the two towers for huge prices
and, thanks to the attacks, the military budget of the United
States
beats all records
at last it'll be possible to have recourse to nuclear arms
at last it'll be possible to embark on new wars
let business thrive !

In the parks, the New Yorkers form into circles
like Indians around their fires
they take one another by the hand and pray.
Are they going to hear the murmur of the dead
of the whole Earth ?

(If they want the words of their prayer to reach the ears
of an all-powerful humanity
they will need to enlarge the circle
and allow the other people of the Earth
the barefoot
the ragged
the under-developed
to take them by the hand
to teach them new songs.)

The War of the Gods

In the beginning was the epic.
The earth was peopled by gods
and the gods made war.
Marduk who had two pairs of eyes
fought against his mother, Tiamat
and her eleven mercenaries,
the Viper, the Dragon, the Mammoth, the giant Lion,
the Mad Dog and the Scorpion Man, led by
      Kingu.
Baal, the king of the air and rain, against Mot, the god
      of drought and Yamm, the god of the sea
and Mot contre Astar,
the little god of irrigation honoured by farmers.
All fought for the control of the heavens
and the control of the earth.
Insufferable band
they spread among men
evils and benefits
catastrophes and victories
and made order and disorder, fear and civilisation
reign on earth.
Then, finally, men
got the better of the first gods.
Today, no-one no longer fears them.
But the new gods,
in spite of their human appearance,
are much more terrifying.
They have much more sophisticated weapons,
guns with infra-red sights,
spy satellites,
self-guiding bombs with auto-directing warheads,
laser beams for surgical strikes,
long distance chemical weapons,

intercontinental nuclear weapons,
tanks armed with depleted uranium,
States and television channels,
Courts, banks,
international organisations,
good reasons and a good conscience...
The universe is nothing but an electronic game for them
where the enemy always rises up again and death
has no meaning.
The new gods unleash storms in
        the desert
and leave behind only charred bodies.
They fight for the control of black gold,
and to impose their laws on others.
As under Hammourabi
men and women are condemned
to slavery for debt
they have a ring put through their nose
and they are sold in public squares.
The new gods bring the reign of disorder,
they corrupt the earth and hearts,
and set peoples at war with one another.
The new gods prepare star wars
the Apocalypse
which the ancients were content to dream about.
Let a new Flood sweep them away
greater than the Flood told about
twenty-five centuries before our era
in the eleventh tablet of the book of Gilgamesh !
And once more let life be saved
by the Arc of solidarity !

Is he good, is he bad?

Diderot is sitting, in his dressing gown, at his desk.
He stops writing for a moment
and rests the quill against his lips.
'Is he good, is he bad ?'
Perhaps he's thinking of his philosopher friends
who are obsessed with this question too.
Rousseau 'the best of men'
the author of Emile, this great sensitive heart,
to whom one would grant absolution without confession
and who put his five children into care.
Or Voltaire, that devil of a man,
the refugee from the chateau of Ferney
this man of sarcasm, this cynic, this misanthrope
who becomes enraged when a certain Calas
who he doesn't even know, suffers an injustice.
'Is he good, is he bad ?'
His play is causing him trouble.
It's the title he'll be most happy with….
The question deserved to be asked.
(Since the gas chambers at least
we know that he's capable
of the worst as of the best).
'Is he good, is he bad ?'
Each time they tried to dismiss it
the question came back through the window
like this fly which comes through the casement
and makes the philosopher raise his head.
What is he thinking about at this moment ?
Perhaps the chambermaid.
(Ah, human nature…)
'Is he good, is he bad ?'
Man is not what he is,
he is what he becomes

He is what he makes of himself.
'Is he good, is he bad ?'
Finally
the reply will only be provided
at the very end
of the performance.

Epode on the Natural Order

To hunt with a cudgel
and to dress themselves in animal skins
was natural for the cavemen.
It had always been so
and it would always be so.
That there were free citizens
having the right to speak freely in the Forum
and labouring or educated slaves
over whom one could have
the right of life or death
was natural for the men of Antiquity
because that was how the City lived in harmony.
(No-one, not even the boldest minds
put it in question).
That humanity should be eternally
divided
between lords and serfs
in conformity with divine law
was just as natural
for the man of the Middle-Ages;
just as crisis and unemployment
are natural for the man of today.
Because what is is natural.
So, the day when capitalism
is replaced
its disappearance too will appear natural.

A Tomb for the Peasants

When he who from dawn to dusk every day
            bends to the earth
lifts his eyes to the sky
and sees the injustices committed in his name
he demands a settling of accounts.

Why must the vassal who feeds monks and knights
die of hunger ?

The lords who are supposed to look after the peasants
pass through the fields, pillage the harvests
and put the country at their mercy.

They impose drudgery, they take the lion's share
            for themselves and don't carry out their duty.

In the woodlands, in a field close to an oak copse
            the peasants have gathered.

Here they are, lord, establishing a parliament
            and forming a commune
- hence the long-standing insult of the term -

Here the beasts of burden, instead of keeping as they should
            their brows bowed to the earth, dare to raise their eyes.

They take hold of their scythes, their sticks
            their pikes
and head for the castles.
But ill befalls those who demand justice of the powerful.

Once the first fears have passed
the lords and their men-at-arms
are going to go hunting peasants like they go to hounds.

They're going to track them through the thickets, encircle
        them in the fields, drive them out of hiding

and massacre them.

They'll plunge them in molten lead or boiling pitch

they'll cook them slowly over small fires.

All the captured will have their hamstrings cut.

They will cut off their ears, tear out their tongues or
        their eyes
so that those pardoned, out of Christian charity
will go into the countryside and wandering in the lanes
will teach others the terror of uprising.

As for the one who claimed to be the king of the peasants,
before
        quartering him, on his head they'll put
a white hot iron crown.
And that is how things were done in the gentle country of
France
in the time of troubadors and courtly love, in the
        northern regions, close to the Norman lands
and the grass that grows sweetly in the breeze
        grows on their bones

and the earth that sleeps, like a pregnant woman,
        fecund every springtime

is soaked in their blood.

Epitaph to the First World War

The poplars - a blue line of infantry - collapse
        on the horizon
as though mown down by cannon.
Here those are fallen who had scarcely risen, unopened buds,
clumps of crushed men, youth
like good earth broken by a ploughshare,
lives turned over for the sterile work of history.
Poppies and cornflowers, here fell a country's youth
mingled with that of another
the edelweiss and the lilac.
Here the earth is held together by hair
blond hair and brown hair mingled.
In the black Chemin des Dames, those who will have had
        no entitlement to the gentleness of women lie in
        the muddy bed of the trenches
the poppies and the lilacs and their loves in the slaughterhouse.
So many hopes, so many inventions and poems which
        will never see the light of day
dreams hung on the butcher's hook
while others in the rear hang their smart overcoats
        on the peg
and go about their little and their big business.
Special promotion: Young soldiers for sale
end of the line - everything must go - stock clearance
surplus men - civilian and military...
these young men who believed they were dying for their country
died for deposit boxes.
They fell that others might remain seated
in their armchairs and on their colonies.

Of them only a half-effaced name remains in the village square
on the monument to the dead
the deceiving monument which represents those who lie in the earth
as if they were rising to the attack
and portrays as victors the vanquished of the war.
On the black ploughed fields of history their blood nevertheless
has given rise to a scarlet dawn.

The Progress of War

In the distant Middle Ages
it sometimes happened
that a king
died on the battlefield.

Later, Napoleon
surveyed the movement of his troops
from the top of a hill…

Today, the generals
follow from their offices
the remote-controlled trajectory of their missiles
which fly - far from where they are - to strike towns
and civilians.

(To avoid the dangers of war
the best thing these days
is to follow
            a military career.)

The Achievements of Capitalism

So this system will have achieved miracles before our very eyes:
under its reign abundance reveals itself the cause of poverty,
progress engenders barbarism,
the strengthening of the State, insecurity
the development of media
under-information,
the scintillating conquests of science
generalised ignorance,
economic globalisation
tribal wars,
the unification of the world market
the division of workers and peoples,
as for artists
all that remains for them
is to produce commodities
and to cultivate ugliness.

Lucy

Lucy, African hominid fossil
that the luck of excavation provides
as being our oldest ancestor
(about 3 million years)

1

I am Kurd Semite Armenian Sumerian Greek Hittite
I am of these exoduses and I walk
in quest driving my flocks far
from the demons which pursue me and assail me
and burn me

2

I am the percussive beatings of heart to body
rhythms which collide with me
Lifting one by one all the successive skins
of the self of the ages
respirations which take it in turns

3

Me Lucy the ultimate recumbent the tall woman
        Africa
first man
skull open to the stars
bent over this Orient which casts me back Mongol
        and Persian
gasping at open spaces

4

These riverbanks weigh on me I will assail the stars
and the suns too
I will track the negro I will confine the Indian I am
the viral weapon the alpha laser the anti cell
the extreme radical

5

I close your eyes in the stench of
mouths made to smile
were you my raw meat lost in a cause
which wasn't mine armed without thinking
come up from deep waters stomach bloated

6

I pine away I stab myself with a sabre
I am a gentle sati eunuch to look after you
I am a galley-slave cotton worker sponge diver
diamond worker sugar worker salt-taxer filth-eater
and prostitute

7

You press yourself against me I hold onto your guts
hidden in this charnel-house
you speak to me in words I can't understand
I thought I recognised you by the last light of dawn
in this stadium

8

I am the kid buried earthquake after earthquake
shrouded in mud
I no longer bleed I dry in the wind
I dry with flies I wipe my rottenness
on my earth on my sand

9

Lucy you look at me petrified insensitive
nonchalantly fixed
as indifferent as night to my fear
Lucy my mother Lucy my sons
inexorable

She Who Walks

She who walks
her ten children spat
together

And the ten bent down seizing
each one the still warm shroud of their father

And yet the mother
her children ten together
sobs

> I took the ten of you
> my children of the five sexes
> my children of the five earths
> and I walked

Because they speakers of races,
of women, would have made their slaves.
Men who love men,
they would have emasculated them.
Women who love women, would have burnt.

Children of the five colours
I snatched you from delirium
and try to find you a safe place
to let your tongues breathe

> In these pains of exodus
> I would like to invent a place
> where you can put down roots
> unburdened of abjection

I spit as far as I can
your poisons and the morgue
howling to counter inheritance

How I would prefer to submerge you
in the ordinariness of calm souls
to entangle your impressions
with the testimonies of belonging

                how I seek
           and have sought places of asylum
      How many walks and hallucinated
                      awakenings

Terrifying assaults
Terrifying refuges

While I walk vomiting

And always in horror of the mutiliated face
of a father

                Teaching you to spit
                And to spit no more

The Name

That God getting decidedly too bored, said:

Let there be hurricanes, earthquakes
volcanoes and floods !

And he called them 'disasters'.

On the second day.
he invented the virus, bacteria, prions
and cells in overdrive
which he called 'agony'.

It was the third day.

Still listless, that God said:

Let there be
famine, massacres
slavery and genocide !

And he added drugs, alcohol and exorbitant interest rates.
And he attributed to them the word "dependence".

On the fourth day,
he invented chemical weapons, the atomic bomb,
land mines and poison gas.

On the fifth day, weighing up what was still missing
he gave birth to
rape,
incest, forced prostitution,
torture and the mafia.

And it was jubilant peace.
And it was the sixth day.

On this sixth day,
truly tired,
that God would have liked to rest
but mulling over his omissions,
he indulged in
imperialism, fascism,
dictatorship, plunder and terrorism.

At last it was the seventh day.

So he sank back into cheerfulness.

However,
struck by the sequential dullness
and inanity of his creations
he wiped them out with one blow
and began again.

Day after day for six days
that God said:

> *Let there be:*
> *irreparable wrong,*
> *alienation,*
> *loneliness,*
> *cynicism,*
> *impotence,*
> *and absolute stupidity !*

On that seventh new day,
in his final smugness
as he contemplated his great work
that God regretted it still lacked
his trademark.

So,
he made in his image
all at once:

> *bile,*
> *the macula,*
> *hands, eyes*
> *and*
> *everything that goes with them.*

And, in the clay, setting down his signature
he offered up His Creation

and called it 'Scandal'.

What do You Know ?

Their stone grafitti
        gasps
at the wind's black kisses
  towards over there which will arrive

Anonymous signatures
        made with fingernails
in improbable countries
     adding nothingness to nothingness

What do you know of revolt
          yes revolt
  of the links of shooting stars
    between the living and the dead
        I have lead you onto these tombs
         these tombs
become strangers in a strange land
       and you have picked flowers
       And what do you know of vertigo
       yes vertigo
  insuperable frontier
    between laughter and pain
        And of unavoidable appeals
     of oblivion
of waves of speech in the pit of the stomach
  of songs of thick night
       The still dazzled soul
   of a tear that has said no
a statue falls asleep at the bottom of the sea
      without casting a glance

With Very Gentle Words

And now
I will have very
gentle words
until my death
to counter my memories

and to no longer dread
the indecent emptiness
when you never know
who will be dogged
by absence

Words
so as no longer to dread
the fear of a tiny child
who will no longer be able to sleep

Very gentle words
to forget
this inability to search
through the ashes
and these wide-eyed wakes
and these irradiated
vomitings

Excuse my anger
for my vengeance
and my camouflage
excuse my mad will
to fossilise beauty
into tainted scrap iron

I will have very gentle words
            until my death
to counter my memories
            and no longer dread
            the obscure shadow
asleep on the rape
            and the despair
                        of mothers

A Charming Little Square

It was Sunday the weather was fine
On the charming little square
Near the mouth of the metro

We were a few friends
Perhaps we knew that morning
We'd need staying power

To sell newspapers that day
And to defend at whatever cost
Freedom of expression

There was a certain whiff of powder
A nervousness about the city
The paras had time on their hands

They came running looking for a fight
Leather gloves on their hands
Carrying truncheons and chains

And blood ran on the tarmac
It was Sunday
It was Sunday
On the charming little square.

The Visit to Bertolt Brecht

Today they told me he wasn't here
Off on his travels again
In exile perhaps here or elsewhere
He's used to it

It's our history which forces us
To live in exile pushed to the margins
Half silence half murmur
Half sun half shadow
Forbidden to have a foot in the future
Watched over by all the professional police
And the amateurs

More painfully than resolutely
Determined to cling to refusal
Distance taken
From daily shame
And the double-dealing of cops and lackeys
Finding our refuge in shame

And in the dignity of being ashamed
About everything done in our name
By the puppets of contempt the tricksters
The criminals with blood on their white hands
The merchants of starvation the killers
Those they call our fellow creatures

Today Bertolt Brecht isn't here
He's living in his books
Perhaps he's preparing the great show
The great cleansing
Weigel isn't here either
Pity

We can hear her voice in spite of everything
Hoarse if fraternally raucous
In the kitchen above her oven
Amongst her culinary inventions her recipes
For strange meals
The whole world in her soup.
All our life has had its share of absence
We've watched the theatre of the world
And its washed out mirror-image
As through a glass

The derisory stuff of days and its cockiness
Weigel isn't in the theatre's canteen either
Where the odour of her tobacco lingers
Here where simmered
Resistance to purblindness its hands over its eyes
To indifference its hand on its heart
Mud and lead in its ears

Am I going to wait for them as in the past
He like a brooding bear
She like humanity's canteen-keeper
I will go to the window
To watch them pass in the peace of the garden
As in the past come back here
     A huge living space
Picasso on the wall
Replays over and over the trump card of peace
The queen of hearts has awoken as a dove
I caress with the end of my finger
A little bit of myself become a silent book
On the shelf
     True we have opened the last volume
The last to appear the great book
Of the great Chronicles of peace
War struts lording it

Face of death it leads a hard life
            Shakespeare his head resting on his ruff
Taps with his foot he thunders
Peace is no small matter
But perhaps the only one that matters
Pen and ink vigils
Nocturnal dialogues
Secret meetings in exile
The apprenticeship of dialectic
I've opened *The Good Person Of Setzuan*
To pass the time
To gain time
At the final page
            Do we need other men ? or a different world ?
            Or other gods ? Unless we can do without them.
            ......Ask yourselves if there's a way
            To help a good soul find the true path
            That we call goodness

Here it's a vast antechamber for work
To work no to die
To work at not dying

You can be busy with a stack of things at once
Those of the day the topicality of days its buffoonery
The poison of words
Crime with real bullets

The other scene the boards
Poetry drama as a riposte
Where the hours and the centuries
Become spokespeople take the rostrum

The typewriter is waiting like me
There will be a sequel
It has simply been covered
Against dust and boredom

Dreams come through the windows
Unpardonable
In the transparent mists of absence

If you denounce the unacceptable
If you protest against it
You enter into exile

You leave the country of the established the staid
Those who fear everything that moves and will move
Before taking a little rest
To live better the following day
Brecht casts a long look at his cane
And his cap hanging on the hook
Which are the provisions for an endless journey
With his attention always alert for a thought
Which refuses to stand fast against stupidity

Before falling asleep he raises his eyes
Towards that photograph
That of the little man deep in thought
His quiet face vaguely smiling
At having understood the route of uncertainty
The good route

It would have been too easy to wallow
In the stagnant pools of dead reason
While day by day in blue ink
The great chronicles of living reason are written
That which affirms and denies itself, that which travels
To listen to other lips other mouths
Arrived from everywhere
From all the transportations
We hear the melodies of anxiety
Amongst the death rattles the harbingers of agonies

With worry
We'll have to endlessly put together
A bouquet of new questions

Open the door to the unknown
To everything which is not forgotten
To everything which will come back from exile.

War Peace

War life betrayed
Life separated from life
Mourning on the flagpoles

War and its most radiant face
We know it and glorify it
This absurd skull with empty sockets
And this plaster sneer

War has only one face
That of ossuaries
Trophies of death

And the unfortunates under mud's uniform
Signed up for fire's ritual
For the spit of powder and lead

Put in line made to march
Graduated for tragedy
For carnage
What remains for the survivors
If not to endlessly scratch the mad image
Ceaselessly garishly retouched

And precisely to understand before the children
How gun carriages bring instability
Why for whom the drums roll

Forsee from their smoke conflagrations as they take

And guess whose hand throws the torch

Before the children before the children.

A Cockstride Into Town

Town alive
In all its stone its flags
All its streets
Not empty
But swarming with slipstreams and silhouettes
Which go their own way towards unimaginable fates

Alive in its avenues
Like rivers between the high cliffs
Of the facades of windows and of deserted balconies

Of boulevards where flows on the finest days
A united crowd which demands to be heard
When the powerful only have ears for themselves
For a little justice
For a little less bastille
Not to forget to be citizens

Who I am where I speak from I need to know
I'm on my way I'm travelling
Bent over the carriageway of centuries
Carrying round my neck the night of slavery
As much as to say unknown in the unknown
Not long ago subjected to being nothing but a ghostly
absence

Buried face discovered face
Who am I
Who are we exactly
What have we become over the centuries
Having been born between paving stones and barricades.

I'm two hundred years old I have hardly
Left the Place de la Bastille
I walk through Paris I'm not alone
I link arms with the dead and the living
Old fierce combatants
Fresh youth

The tramping of centuries in space
O the slowness of the rabble's arrival in the world
Yesterday I was at the foot of a thick wall
A prison
And I cried that jails must be opened
Prisoners given the sky and the earth
A people delivered
I have just left the Place de la Bastille
It was a grave and joyous day of change
I walk arm in arm with this living crowd
A crowd in which each finally lifts his face
A new face

I was I recall at one
With those who storm bastilles
From this Paris of boulevards I've seen
Morbid monarchies
Princes of terror
Grow pale
Pettinesses and great tyrannies collapse

I have seen I have other eyes for seeing the world
I have changed my skin my blood
Suddenly as if I had been born adult

As if I had acquired once and for all
My new stature my citizen's demeanour
Another way of being
An existence
Different in every way
Different finally for having fellow creatures.

I'm moulded from the flesh of the dead and the living
By day to day history
And its century to century insights
Reclaimed worked fertilised to my roots
Enhanced in the dignity of living
By the noble words of laws

I walk in step with the old fighters of the past
I have walked on the paving stones of barricades
It's true that all men are equal before the law
I climb onto the knees
Of the statue of the Republique
In the July sun in Paris
And joyously throw in the air my *bonnet phrygien*

Slowly I conquered the territories of the word
To speak and to write was the privilege of the powerful
They defend it tooth and diamond nail
With whatever violence and wealth you like

I can no longer be satisfied with the dried flowers
Of writing

I can no longer strip myself
Of this conquered tongue inherited
From the high handed by tough struggle
I can no longer take pleasure in
The obscure prattle
Of childhoods and solitudes

I walk through the Paris of streets
An entire history beneath an open sky
With its dramas and its enigmas
I try to be worthy of Paris
My town my citizen's city
So much water has flowed under the bridges of the Seine

So much blood in the streets
So much blood on the walls
As far as the edge of tombs

I like this town and its urban speech
The streets and their shop windows
The inaccessible luxury and the market stall
Where money and smiles of all kinds
Are exchanged

I walk in the Paris of libraries
Of cinemas and theatres
Reading is a path towards yourself and towards others
The theatre is a great matter of public utility
I walk arm in arm with the dead and the living
There are some dead who were more alive
Than those who live and are content to be individuals

I walk through Paris
There is so much beneath each step
Fragments of life splendours of history
Wiped out by ignorance and ingratitude
But I very much like the architecture of the scaffolding
Shining in the sunlight

I have walked through Paris and it's the month of May
I stop
At a flower stall
I will take some flowers over there to the wall.

The Oradour School

Jean we two enrolled
In the Oradour school
Sat down in the ashes of Oradour

Wrote by wetting our fingers
With the charred dust
Of the ashes of Oradour

And all the words took on a resonance
            And barbarism
And refusal of barbarism
The satchel was heavy You said
Jean 'with all the aggravating circumstances
Of reality' we had to overcome

Oradour was for us a path of harsh light
The satchel was heavy we carried
Spit balls
Wood bowlines nails
For the great scaffolding of happiness

In the Oradour school we learned
To breathe the animal's air
Its breath its stink affronted us
'We have known Evil on earth'
You said Jean

We had to reinvent a vocabulary of refusal
Disobedience to the sad education
Of the masters and the false prophets
They wanted to muzzle us to beat us
But we laughed we two up our sleeves
In spite of the cold
In the Oradour school there was neither god nor
                                        master

From the Cliff Top

Wave after wave
You can see the tide remaking
The sea-front

There are eddies
Whirlpools

But like the sea
Freedom knows no rest.

Legend of the International Brigades

Float like a dawn scarf
Over this twentieth century coming to its end
Full of fury and noise
Black with wars, killing and horror

Float like a dawn scarf
Simple and pure like the taste of liberty
Simple like the elementary idea of justice
The epic lived on a global scale
That of the Volunteers for Spain

And let scrupulous history, for an instant,
Forgetting unresolvable quarrels
Step aside
Let it bow before the legend, before
Each of these flesh and blood men

Each of those who, looking at his hands
Lay down his tools
And alone with his most secret thoughts
With the bitter sadness of going far away
Measured his courage to leave his loved ones
Finalised at once the proud plan of his departure
As if he had henceforth only one duty

That of those men
All alone behind the secret of his brow
And deaf to the platitudes of indifference

Set off to find out
If a hand
In another hand
Is a good defence
Against despair and unhappiness

Each of those set off from home
Poor and ill equipped
Who was soon a hundred
Thousands and thousands
Tens of thousands
Hundreds of thousands going to find out
Set off to join a people in battle
Attacked
In their own land
By their country's army
Set off to help a republic
Prey to assassins

Crossing spaces
Scaling mountains
Crossing seas and oceans

Making a way through
Bad tempered bureaucracies
Breaking all boundaries
Escaping from the police
Trespassing on the smugglers' routes

Thousands and thousands
On converging roads
Come to offer a helping hand
To life to death
To a whole people poor and ill-equipped
Ground down by a war called civil

I will shoot half of Spain
If I have to
Said General Franco

Come in their thousands
Not proud but humble
Not glory-seekers
Nor profiteers
Nor manipulators

Not warriors but fighters
For liberty defying death
Their fists raised aloft
To tell with five fingers
The united hopes for a peaceful world

Rebels dreaming of revolution in the early hours
To be done with the bric-a-brac of unhappiness
Their hands had known only tools
Those of the factory and the land
They demanded only weapons

Fighting against the morgue and contempt
Face to face with the ferocity of hordes
Good for the front
Good for shooting
Good for the charge and the attack

Good for strategies
And even for the absence of strategies
Good for the last stand
Where the honour of living blends
With that of dying

Brigades of a humbly lucid courage
Illuminating shady tricks
Flying in the face of purblind disaster
Against the fatal combinations
Of all pusillanimous powers

O far-sighted Brigades
Come to bar the way to the spectre of war
To take on the sowers of discord
And if possible
To put out once and for all the torches of evil
The future world conflagration

O visionaries
It's only in the mouths of phoney warriors
That the vanquished are always wrong
Witterings of a passing victor giving himself airs

But you were right
Whoever was against or with you
To rise up in the face of the huge crime

You were you
Vision and reason
The future soon enough
Too late alas
Proved you right

The Coefficient of Failure : Notebook 12

Savages are sometimes very savage.

A savage in a very savage state can commit very savage spontaneous acts.

A very savage savage is not always peaceable and is not at all poetic.

His very savage state is often a state of combat.

A savage combatant goes to war. Without knowing it, given it's his condition. A very savage condition.

War is sudden, brutal and rapid.

Because the very savage state doesn't last.

It's a touch (of humour), a bout (of moodiness), an acceleration.

The very savage savage becomes once more simply savage without knowing it.

Sometimes the non-savage believe they've been victims of a savage in a very savage state.

Because a very savage savage speaks a savage language. A language which protests, which shouts. A language which demands too.

So the very savage savage is leaping ahead. Or making a kind of gesture.

A gesture like an extract from a dance. But not really. Rather a gesture as a fragment of combat.

Whoever is at the end of the leap or the gesture can feel wounded.

Because he has heard or read the language which protests, shouts, and demands too - savages' language. Gesture language - fragement of combat.

And because he doesn't know this language.

As for himself, a savage, after the gesture, begins dancing at once and starts laughing. Then replies in savage language.

The Coefficient of Failure : Notebook 14

The savages are amongst us.

A savage can be in a condition of resistance.

A condition-of-resistance-savage is due, for example, to the confrontation between the savage and a non-savage situation or condition.

The condition-of-resistance-savage knows how to say no.

He often says no.

He's against.

He's against clichés.

He's opposed to what's imposed.

He's opposed to languages, thinkers, imposed actions.

It's important not to forget that language-thinking-doing are a single and same act for the savage.

Thinking means saying what's to be done as strictly as possible.

Doing means thinking the language or writing of saying or doing.

Or writing the doing of saying.

Language – or 'languaging' in savage – is saying or writing the thinking of doing, doing the thought, thinking the doing.

Or thinking the doing of saying. Or thinking the saying of doing.

The Lovers

Each morning the 7.01 nude crosses the corridor.
He, from the kitchen, turns his eyes
in order to catch this flash in flight.
The marvel accomplished, the footprints
evaporating from the tiles, he drinks his coffee
and has no difficulty
in imagining Sisyphus happy

Silence and Dust

Who, beneath the pallor of the flesh
with the silhouette such an horrendous outline
would identify the pretty blonde
celebrating her results, in bare feet in front of the Syringas ?
Certainly not her, three kids later
when going out as a couple, says the woman in the deli,
you can count it on your fingers….
YOU -CAN- COUN-TIT-ON-YOUR-FIN-GERS !

Poor Tropics

Each time he returns, he beeps and beeps
outside the block of flats,
so that his wife and children will unload the boot,
carry in the shopping of meat and veg.
Under the balconies, with the dog barking,
he feels pride fill his chest,
the pride of the victorious hunter,
as the clamour for such-and-such a shampoo,
the approbation of the tribe
confirm him in his role and magnify
his incredible skill.

Low Tide

At the foot of the towers
which will perhaps become shallows,
rehoused like a hermit-crab
in a temporary shell,
she has just enough room
for her family pictures and a third of her furniture.
The rest is going mouldy
while at the window
she warms her deformed hands.

Ground Level

for Leslie Kaplan

A bar with a bleached floor, green walls
whose customers are intent on virtual racing.
Old timers, elbows on the table…
Youngsters, in front of whom no woman walks...
Once inside, you hear
Love songs, disappointing results.
You guess that audible
The voices would be excessively shrill….

Homage To Kundera

Woolly hat and parka
here he comes with his hands in his pockets.
For years we've seen him
defending day against night,
invoking what rears up
with a glimmer of Marat in his bath.
And yet, he's done all the evil he could
and his shadow betrays
more than (ancient) hunger or widowhood.
When death appears straight and brown in his suit,
why feel sorry for himself ?
he will simply go chasing dogs.

From a Mirage

In the middle of the afternoon

This ageless Arab

Who returns to the flock

The trolleys

Scattered across

The deserted car park

From a Cantata

You take the ticket, the tyres squeak

The headroom asks its question

You wonder what use

Bach could have been

Before

The invention of underground car parks

Song of Pandemic

First of all, it's a drunkard
Who suffers and who shouts in the streets,
Between the rows of semis
And the blocks of flats…

Next, it's a man who has lost
His son ? His dog ? And who calls
Across the neighbourhood,
So that people come out to help him….

Finally, it's the Reaper
Who enjoins to swell,
At once, the exponential procession !
The Reaper with a thousand lures:

Adolescent rowdyism,
Kinfe-grinders' old tales,
The miaowing of cats (indistinguishable
from the cry in the night of babies)…

Zone

When she wakes, the brick
warehouses and the tall chimney,
like the pain in her finger, have disappeared.
But there has been no kiss.
On the island, in the middle of the river,
stretches a gulf
where the seagulls are leaves
snatched alive from a typewriter.

Relationship (s) V1

Orlando has always taken notes in a hand as stylish as his tie.

And convoluted. Orlando takes notes in order to have a hold on the world and to control cause and effect.

Emergence depends on an observer.

On the other hand, Stephanie prefers to insert pipettes into test tubes.

To each his truth.

'You see what I mean ?' = consensus.

from Southern Hemisphere

all the birches are in line
animals in a field, they're sheep
the trunks vibrate
a belfry
lights on already
lorries on the parallel motorway
green, some greens
a toll
all the houses facing the same way
the sun ?
a square cemetery with graves arranged in squares

a bell tower
a tractor
a pylon
headlights
a cottage
night
black

from That life is a Dream

I dream of a world where Glenn Gould would be the name
of a porno actor
A world of before or after. (Perhaps after.)
Commodities would have their own life.
All the girls would wear sexy short nightdresses and would rush
down hills as they sang.
They would say: 'Oh Jack'....
Addiction, whatever that is, would no longer be pernicious.

I dream of a world which would play my music
in its every detail.

What We Have Gained from Bourgeois Democracy is at Least to Have Saved Our Precious Pair of...
CUCKOOETTES !!!

(Title no. 1, side A)

for Laurent C

We are no longer, o thank god, under a regime similar to that
of the Stuarts
when,

in 1664,

an English editor by the Namje of John Twyn was
arrested judged,
emasculated in public,

hung,

quartered
and his limbs nailed to the doors of the citad--------------------------
--el
and on London Bridge.

His crime was to have

upset   the   royal
power

by publishing a pamphlet

where he
argued

that people had

the right to revolt against a gove
rnment which

oppressed them...

The Disturbances in the Publishing Sector, the Sale of Guns, the Tycoon and Others...

(Title n 2, side B)

(To illustrate our song, let's take the example of the publisher *La Decouverte* who took over the lamented *Francois Maspero* house. In a few years this had moved from the hands of the 'new realist" CFDT to those of the Havas Agency, then to those of Vivendi to end up in those of Hachette/ Lagardere. Finally, ownership has recently fallen to the De Wendel group whose chief is the tycoon Ernest/Antoine Seilliere LE GRAND PATRON OF MEDEF & CO....Symbolic, n'est-ce pas ?)

SyMBOLLOCKS
(...almost a remake !)

&to look down on still & always a little more Hegel
By defenestrating with Diogenes the Cynic
From the height of the World Trade Centre
A luxury hen and a sturgeon's egg
To see which will arrive first
In the Great Race to the Stars.............
(Georges Hassomeris, D.33)
......a Sophie Nivet,

& to hark back in reverse slang
24H in 24 (Through the stars)
Palindromes, radar, kayak & to faf

& to relocate to Hong/Kong
To manufacture poems
(Lyrico/Lyrical...) on the assembly line

& To realise all at once
That the sprinkling of the multiple
is a moment of unity in movement

& to uncover with H/Ball and R/Huelsenbeck
The neo/Nazi who is dozing
Behind every romantic poet

& to have been like everyone *37 years ago*
A German Jew to become finally today
A Palestinian of the PLO

&
To no longer work except
On the 1st May

& to run that day
The stall of the absolute
In the infinite

& to want to change the world
But to admit to being ABSOLUTELY unable
To put up with one's neighbour

& to find a Turkish slipper on your foot
When putting paper
On a level with your mouth

& to startle (Again and always a little+) the COMMERCIAL
onlookers
                by hell
eliminiating Ben Vautier (Before he gets fatter...)
into a can of Campbell's soup

&
not to like god but
Women

& to roam like beauty in the street

With ALWAYS (At least…)
A fit of mad laughter's lead on the Mona Lisa's smile

& to offer a tin of ungarnished sauerkraut
To Mme Bovary while murmuring in her ear:
Mme Bovary, the dressing, it's me !

& to suddenly declare with Aragon:
Woman is man's future…
EXCEPT FOR THE ARLESBIAN !

& to titillate the huge black hole of the Galaxies
With the digit of the lightning that guides
The world

& to take (At least three times a week)
TOTALLY TOTAL poetry hostage
In the simple & noble goal of emptying your balls

& to note with DADA
That it's Francois Rabelais
Who's beating Pasquier

& to enter (Somewhere between the end of silents
& the beginning of the talkies) one ear &
Come out of the other

& to hire in English
(Which is the language of commerce)
your labour to a Lord

& to lean on your leanings
Like Proteus on his bottle
Or on Diogenes's barrel

& to attain to the absolute quintessence of
TOTALLY TOTAL poetry

& to realise…(Suddenly !) that it isn't a solution

& to have like Rimbaud the blue/White eye
The narrow brain (& awkwardness in struggle !)
Of your Gaulo/Gallic ancestors

& to realise suddenly that the Mycenian isn't
(For me !) A subject of study like any other, but
THE LANGUAGE OF MY FORBEARS

& to take very seriously your new role of 'Planet'
(At the precise moment when Descartes invents Analytical
geometry)

& to tidy up epistemological pessimism
(Which is a rotten fantasy of idealism)
At the lowest level of becoming aware

& to massacre with a chain saw a huge forest of Bonsais
To harm the little editor of your
Humble servant

&
To deplore with Rabelais the sadly notorious:
Transition from the wine service to the divine service

& to find very
Very aesthetic the old coats of arms a/
Dored restored of the ethic (……Music !)

What is Poetry?

OTHER EXAMPLES:
[But, I repeat, there are no archetype(s)…]

……for Bouvard & Pecuchet

Thus, the interiority of the subject discovering in himself
A deeper presence than him/Self, it's saint Augustin

The analysis of poetic language
As the sole locus of the revelation of being, it's M.Heidegger

The transposition into grandiose visions
Of an inexhaustible interior secret transposed to the height
Of an aristocratic communication, it's Saint/John/Perse

Metaphysical humour
Which changes the very conditions of being
By the aggressions of the language which names it, it's Michaux

The conscientitious press attaché
disciplined enough to deserve a promotion
to the Romanian Embassy in Vichy in 1942, it's Ionesco

The psychology of homo religiosus
Arriving at the profane by way of the sacred, it's Regis Debray
Carnal nature represented by grass, it's Rene Char

The flight out of time
& refuge in religion and myths
Which constitute the sum of useful knowledge, it's Mircea Eliade

The validation of the negationist Jean Plantin's university
diplomas
(The day of the 60th anniversary of the arrest of Jean Moulin in
Caluire),
It's the Lyon administrative court
'Jean Moulin is dead for a second time', it's the Marc/Bloch
Circle

'Poetry which sees itself as conferring a sacerdotal dimension
& which won't give way to despotism except to dress itself in
chance,
Retire to the heights - SELF FLAGELLATE - and escape torpor'

It's Dominique de Villepin

Poetry for sados/Masos, it's the Others
'Every poet who isn't dead at thirty is an incompetent !'
It's once again & always.....Dominique de Villepin

'A good poet is a dead poet !', it's the Others

The Marine Cemetery, it's Paul Valery
The merry cemetery, it's Bernard Heidsieck

Poetry which turns religion to mockery with
The weapons of (dicey) reason,
It's Lucien de Samosate

Poetry which is art
Desacralisation pushed to its limit,
It's taboo

Clear thinking is the height of perfection & wisdom is telling the truth & acting according to nature

......for Mumia abou Jamal

BEAUTY IS IN THE STREET followed by I IS OF THE
NOTHERS

Beauty is an aborigine from nowhere
& her statue a poem which won't stay in one place
& seeing it needs about 20 bison skins to make a tepee
Beauty leaves her reserve her beautiful face painted the colour of
        indiscipline
She leaves the centre of the old amphitheatre
In which she lived as a recluse
Somewhere between Lourdes & Eurodisney
To go and dance on the rose of the winds
With the sun in her hands & all the world's ways
Unfasten their laces when she passes
Beauty who is an aborigine
Of all kinds doesn't choose God
IN OTHER WORDS A NEW CHARNEL-HOUSE TO ROT IN
But full and complete Humanity
In the mad, gaudy fair of the great planetary village
Beauty who is a sex bomb of all kinds
Bursts out laughing as soon as she's enticed
She has easy ease and so much the better beauty which passes
& repasses from country to country without ever settling down
IS AN OCEAN OF BIRDS & THE LAUGH OF THE PANTHER
Beauty with in addition and always at least
A fit of mad laughter ahead of Mona Lisa's smile
Beauty which holds out her hand to us with an elegance
& a surprising rapidity the still of real life
To drink to the world's health

By now taking us along with her
In a mad cosmopolitan farandole across the stars
To finally establish that everywhere
Men & women are the same

'We must also liberate the stars'
The last words of Alekos, shot by the Nazis.

Comrades, We Are All Concerned !!!

for Ben V

This poem will no doubt pass 100 metres over the heads
of some, but if we don't try,
a disaster certainly won't be avoided…
especially since we are ALL concerned !!!
The Brazilian congress is now voting for a plan
which will reduce the Amazon Forest to 50% of its size…
This action will take you 1 MINUTE, but please:
AS TIME IS SHORT,
Carve your name immediately on a tree trunk
& send it in the post to your friends !!!
The area to be deforested represents 4 times the size of
Portugal
& would be used principally for agriculture
& for grazing animals.
All the wood is to be sold on the international markets
by big multinational companies
in the form of planks
…to make books and magazines !
Today more than 160 000 square metres
shorn for the same reason are abandoned
& have set in train a process of desertification.
Deforestation and the production of timber at this rate
release into the atmosphere enormous amounts of carbon
adding to the greenhouse effect and climatic changes:
We cannot allow this to continue!!!
AS A FORM OF PROTEST, please copy this poem,
carve your full name on a tree trunk
and then send the lot by post
to everyone you know

(ABOVE ALL DON'T SIMPLY HAVE YOUR TREE TRUNK FORWARDED BY WRITING 'PLEASE FORWARD' or 'PLEASE PASS ON' IN ORDER TO AVOID ROWS OF HUNDREDS OF THOUSANDS OF USELESS NAMES WHICH WOULD REQUIRE THE MANUFACTURE OF AN EXTRA BOOK <u>this is urgent!!!</u>...AS TIME IS SHORT!!!

(to be continued)

In the Beginning Was the Verb !

.....and so on and to be continued

SEE ROME & DIE !
GO TO HEC (+VIVENDIS) & DIE !
BITE A WIDOW & DIE !
PAINT WITH YOUR FEET & DIE !
TALK WITH YOUR HAIR & DIE !
OPEN THE DEBATE & DIE !
CLOSE THE WINDOW & DIE !
SHOOT YOUR HIGH HORSE &DIE !
BUY A VAN GOGH & DIE !
SING OFF-KEY & DIE !
PISS IN A VIOLIN & DIE !
METAMORPHOSE A PURE VIEW OF THE MIND & DIE!
BUY A THANKSGIVING & DIE !
SAY LITTE & DIE !
SPEAK WELL & DIE !
TALK FOR THE SAKE OF TALKING & DIE !
BE QUIET & DIE !
DIE & DIE !
HAVE & DIE !
BE & DIE !
HAVE BEEN & DIE !
BE AND HAVE BEEN & DIE !
CALL A CAT A CAT & DIE !
BREAK UP YOUR ESSENTIAL SELFHOOD & DIE !
SPEND ALL YOUR SAVINGS & DIE !
SPEAK TO A WALL & DIE !
DIVIDE AND RULE & DIE !
READ & REREAD YOUR BIO/BIBLIO & DIE !
CHANGE WATER INTO WINE & DIE !
CHANGE LEAD INTO GOLD & DIE !
CHANGE A DONKEY INTO A THOROUGH/BRED & DIE !
GO TO THE LIMIT OF THE LIMIT OF THE LIMIT & DIE !

MEASURE ALL THE DISTANCE
THAT STILL HAS TO BE TRAVERSED & DIE !
HIDE YOUR HEAD IN THE SAND & DIE !
CHANGE THE WORLD & DIE !
KNOW yourself AT LAST & DIE !
CRY IN THE DESERT & DIE !
BE QUIET IN THE TOILET & DIE !
TRAMPLE A BUNCH OF WITTICISMS
AT THE FOOT OF A LETTER & DIE !
REPLACE THE OBJECT BY THE CONCEPT,
THE CONCEPT BY THE IDEA OF THE CONCEPT….& DIE !
STAND UP STRAIGHT
AGAINST ESTABLISHED ORDER & MORALITY & DIE !
SUFFER TO BE BEAUTIFUL & DIE

(to be continued)

Biographies

Francis Combes was born in 1953. He has published fifteen books of poetry, two novels, anthologies and translations. He is the moving force behind the publishing house Le Temps des Cerises. He lives in Aubervilliers with his wife, the journalist, Patricia Latour and his family.

Francoise Coulmin lives in Normandy. She is a painter and geographer as well as a poet. She has published five collections in which she explores what it means to be human through the familiar and the remote and expresses her revolt against the evils of the world and insults to human dignity.

David Dumortier was born in 1967 and lives in Paris where he works in psychiatry. He has lived in Syria. He has published several collections and has appeared in many reviews and works frequently in schools. In addition to his writing he is also a photographer.

Jacques Gaucheron was born in 1920. Both his parents were primary school teachers. He spent much of his childhood in Chartres. A veteran of the French artistic milieu he was involved with Aragon and Eluard. He lives in Frette in a house he built himself.

Georges Hassomeris describes himself as a visually cacaphonique meta-Greek and crypto-Dadaist. He was a scholar of classical Greek and Latin but later took up card games. He is a member of the BoXoN review group and has turned towards the web being a fan of visual poems, blogs and discussion groups.

Laure Limongi was born in 1976 in Bastia and now lives in Paris. She has published six collections of poetry and in addition to her readings and lectures has begun on-line projects.

Gerard Noiret was born in 1948. After leaving school he held jobs in various factories before becoming involved with the literary journal *Esprit*. He was involved with Quinzaine Litteraire, has published in many journals and in addition to his writing, lectures frequently and is a regular cultural commentator on French radio.

Veronique Vassiliou was born in 1962 and has published more than twenty books. She is a member of the editorial committee of the political review Poetic Action. She also helped establish the review OEI.